Social Media Marketing a Strategic Guide

Learn the Best Digital Advertising Approach & Strategies for Boosting Your Agency or Business with the Power of Facebook, Instagram, YouTube, Google SEO & More

By Sean Buttle

Table of Contents

Introduction

Congratulations on downloading *Social Media Marketing a Strategic Guide* and thank you for doing so.

The following chapters will discuss everything that you need to know to finally get your social media plan off the ground. There are very few businesses who will succeed in our modern business world if they do not have a good marketing plan that includes some social media. Your customers are online, and they are looking for you there. If you are not present in the right places at the right times (and this includes on social media), then your customers are going to find someone who is.

This guidebook is going to spend some time looking through the steps that you need to take in order to work with social media and to gain the best results in the process. We will explore why social media is so important, before diving into all of the different social media sites that are out there, and how to use each one to your own benefit!

Inside, we will explore organic and paid advertising techniques, along with who should use, all of the major social media sites like Facebook, Instagram, Google, Twitter, YouTube, LinkedIn, and more! While your marketing campaign may not include all of these all of the time, knowing how they work and who will benefit from them the most is going to make a big difference in how well you respond to them, and the results that you are going to be able to get in the process.

Now marketing campaign is complete without using some social media in there, and many companies choose to have two or three social media sites that they spend time with. There are so many things that you are able to do on these sites, and so many ways that you are able to interact and connect with your customers like never before. When you are ready to start increasing your own social media presence, and you are ready to really showcase your products and se your sales and business grow, make sure to check out this guidebook to learn how to get started!

There are plenty of books on this subject on the market, thanks again for choosing this one! Every effort was made to ensure it is full of as much useful information as possible, please enjoy!

Chapter 1: The Importance of Social Media

As a business, it is important to take a look at all of the different options you have available when it comes to advertising and getting your message out there. Not all of the avenues that are available are going to work for your specific needs. While there are many choices, some will work better for local businesses, some will work best for bigger companies, and some will work better for a variety of different reasons. Knowing your own target market, and having a good idea on who you would like to reach can really ensure that you don't waste your marketing money on campaigns that don't work for your needs.

One avenue that you may want to explore when it comes to your market campaign is social media. Social media is taking over the world, and no matter what kind of product you sell, it is likely that you will be able to find a good portion of your customers on one social media platform or another. And since there are so many options to pick from, and many of them are very affordable to advertise and market on, it is worth your time to check them out.

There are a lot of different benefits to adding at least a little social media to your marketing budget. You will be able to reach more of your customers, can increase how much loyalty there is to your brand, and you can reach your customers were they actually are. Some of the other benefits that you are going to enjoy when you start with your own social media campaign includes:

Increased brand recognition

Every chance that you are able to syndicate the content that you want to use, and increase your visibility to the public is going to be valuable. Your social media networks, the ones that you choose to focus on for a bit, are just going to be new channels for the content and the voice of your brand. This is important because it is going to make you easier and more accessible for the customers while making you more recognizable and familiar to the customers you already have. Both of these are going to do wonders for helping your business grow to new heights.

For example, maybe you have a user who is on Twitter quite a bit and they hear about your company wen they stumble on it in a newsfeed. A customer who may be considered apathetic might become more familiar with your brand when they start to see it on several networks, rather than just occasionally on one.

More brand loyalty

According to one report that was recently published by Texas Tech University, brands who spend time being engaged on their various social media channels are going to enjoy a higher amount of loyalty from their customers. This means that, if you are able to, you need to take advantage of all the different tools that social media will give you when it is time to connect with your audience.

You may find that having an open and strategic kind of social media plan could be so important when it comes to morphing consumers to being loyal to your brand. If you find that you are struggling with getting people to not only try out your brand and your products, and to actually stick with you over the long term, then it is time to start a social media strategy if you don't have one, and improve one if you have a strategy in place.

More chances to convert your consumers

Every time you put a post on social media, it is going to present you with a chance to convert some of your customers. when you start to build up the following that you need on social media, you are, at the same time, gaining access to some new customers, some old customers, and some recent customers. And these posts allow you to interact with all of them. Every image, video, blog post, or comment that you share gives you another chance for someone to react. And each of these reactions could potentially lead to someone visiting your site and maybe even with them making a purchase.

Now, this doesn't mean that each and every interaction that occurs with your brand is going to be a conversion. But, every time that there is a positive interaction there, this means that the likelihood of them doing an eventual conversion goes up. Even if you notice that the rates of click through are pretty low, the sheer number of chances of meeting with customers, past, present or future, is going to be higher than anywhere else.

Increased traffic

Without the help of social media, the amount of inbound traffic that you are going to bring into your business is going to be limited down to just those who are familiar with the brand from other sources, and individuals who are searching for the keywords that you took the time to rank. Every social media account that you are able to add to this will mean that there is another path that goes back to your website, and every piece of content that you add to the social media profile means that it is going to give you a new opportunity for a brand new visitor to come and see your website.

Of course, you need to take some precautions with this. Just because you have a social media site doesn't mean that you are going to automatically get the new customers that you would like. You need to be willing and able to post content on a regular basis, keep the content high quality and consistent, and you need to interact in the right way with your customers. If you are able to bring all of these things together on your social media profile, then this means that you are going to be able to really see some great results with the amount of traffic that starts to head to your website.

Lower marketing costs

One of the things that you are going to love the most about social media marketing is that it can be really efficient, while decreasing the amount of costs that you pay to market your brand and products. According to Hubspot, 84 percent of marketers found that they could spend only six hours each week on their social media accounts in order to see an increased amount of traffic.

When you think about the big picture, and how much you spend on the other marketing avenues that you choose to go with, six hours is not that much. You can spend just an hour a day doing this, coming up with a strategy and developing the content, and then you would start to see some of the results that come with your efforts.

Even when you are focusing more on paid advertising with Facebook and Twitter, your costs are going to stay pretty low. Both of these are going to be inexpensive, and you can have a lot of control over how much you spend on these based on your own goals. For example, many marketers start small to see how things go and to get a feel from the work, and then they build up from there based on how the trial run went.

Better rankings on a search engine

As many companies already know, SEO is going to be one of the best ways that you are able to capture the kind of traffic that you want from search engines. But the requirements that are needed to ensure that you are successful with SEO are always changing. It is no longer enough for a company to just update their blog, ensure optimized title tags, and meta descriptions.

Instead, you have to go through and add in a lot of other things as well. But the good news is that you can work with social media accounts and help to increase your rankings. Being active on your social media account, making sure that you interact with others, and producing some high quality content is often going to be a great way for you to really grow your presence online and to get the traffic that you want through SEO.

Better insights about your customers

And finally, the last benefit that we are going to talk about when it comes to social media is that it is going to help you gain some really valuable information about your customers, how they behave, and what they are the most interested in. for example, it is possible that you would go through all of the comments to figure out the way that others think and talk about your business.

Based on the information that you can gather on your customers through these social media sites, you may be able to segment them out based on topic and see which types of content seem to bring in the most interest, and then you will want to produce more of that content over time. You can measure the conversions that happen based on the different types of promotions that you try, and eventually, you are going to find the perfect combination to help you generate the revenue that you want.

As you can see, there are a lot of reasons that many businesses want to work with social media. It does not cost a lot of money for you to get started with this kind of campaign, and it is going to help you to best reach your customers where they are located at the time. When you are able to really work to come up with a good social media strategy, then you are going to be able to really see the growth that you want in your business and with your sales.

Chapter 2: Which Social Media Platform Is the Best?

The first question that you need to ask yourself is which of the social media platforms is going to be the best for your marketing needs. You may look at them and think they are all amazing and that you should spend time on each and every one. While they all have a lot of customers and a lot of things that are unique about them that will make them stand out from the crowd, remember that you do not need to advertise on each one. Your customers are not going to be found on each one, and spreading yourself this thin can be hard.

So, how are you supposed to know which ones are the best for you? This chapter is going to help you out with this by providing a brief overview of some of the most common social media sites that you can work with, how they work, and which kinds of businesses they are going to work the best with. For most customers, you will find that working with two or maybe three of these options is going to be enough. This will help you to use your money and time efficiently while still reaching as many customers as possible. Some of the best social media sites for you to consider will include:

Facebook

For many people, the number one social media site that they are going to use to help them market to their potential customers and earn more sales is through Facebook. Facebook is considered king when it comes to working online, and with billions of active users who spend several hours or more a day online, this is definitely a spot where you are going to find a lot of your potential customers as well.

While not every business is going to concentrate their efforts fully on Facebook, especially if they have a very niche market that seems to be present in another social media site, it is still a great place where you should spend at least a little bit of time. There are a lot of people found on Facebook, many options for advertising, and so much more.

We will get into how to market on Facebook a bit more later on, but you will find that it is a great option to help you earn a good amount of customers. you can use organic advertising and traditional paid advertising as well based on how you want to reach your customers, and so much more. Facebook is a place where you can find even your niche customers, which makes it the perfect option to help you no matter how big or small your audience is at the time.

Facebook is a great option to go with because there is just so much that you can work with. There is a large audience, and many companies have been able to grow their presence on there with just organic reach. This means that their marketing budget was low, outside of the person or team they hired to keep the social media site up and running.

If you already have a good presence online and your business has grown, then Facebook is going to be an easy place to start. A lot of your customers are already there, they are interested in learning about you, and some may already search for you online, making growing your reach easier than you can imagine. You still need to be present and make sure that you respond to them, post valuable content, and be consistent, but growing your following will be easier.

However, for those companies who are not large and well-known, the ones who are just getting started with themselves, much less their social media presence, there is still a lot of room for growth when it comes to Facebook. Both through organic reach and paid advertising, you will be able to reach the customers you want in no time. And since Facebook is such a large and growing network with customers based throughout the world, you are sure to be able to find the right customers for your needs, no matter how you decide to split up your target market.

Instagram

Instagram is the world of pictures and images. The majority of what you are going to see when you work on this social media site is a lot of pictures from companies and individuals all over the world. In fact, while you are able to add some ad copy and words to the pictures, the individual is going to be presented with the picture first, and then they have to go through and actually click on the image to see more.

If your business could really benefit from the use of images to showcase your work or your product, then you really need to work with Instagram as much as possible. Images are the rule when it comes to this social media site, and the higher quality, and the more creative you are able to make those images, the more you are going to get your potential customers interested in what you are doing and what you have available for sale.

In addition to working on the best pictures possible, it is also an option for you to use hashtags and other little additions to make it easier for your potential customers to find you. With some compelling copy, a good link in your bio (Instagram won't allow you to add the links to the individual pictures), working on a few relationships with the right people online, and the right hashtags so potential customers can find you, and you have the recipe for success on Instagram.

Instagram is going to work the best if you are looking to rely on a lot of imagery to sell your product or service. In fact, it is possible to have quite a few followers who won't even look at the words that you post on your site. They will be drawn in by the good visuals. Then, when they finally see something that they like, they may be enticed to push on your website link and check it out.

This doesn't mean that you should not spend some time on the copy that you add in. And the hashtag is going to be super important to make sure that new and existing followers and customers are able to find you when they need to. Having good and compelling copy with the right tags is going to help you so much. But the most important thing to focus on when you spend your marketing budget on Instagram is the imagery and the videos that you decide to post.

Google

Google is a great social media site for you to work on when you need to grow your SEO and help more people find you through search engine queries and more. There are a lot of times when your potential customers are going to find you online. They will put in some kind of keyword search online, and then if you match up with it, then this is going to get the to your website, helping you to get a good sale.

The better your SEO campaign and work, the more customers you are going to get to your website. And the more that you are able to get people to the website, the more potential sales that you are able to get. SEO is important for every kind of business, but if you rely a lot on your website traffic or another website like a blog, then the Google social media marketing is going to be the choice that you will want to spend your time with.

Many businesses are going to be able to see benefits when it comes to working on their SEO, so adding a bit of this to your work is going to make a big difference. Even if you just put a small part of your budget towards this, it is going to give you some big results, and can really be enhanced when you are working with some of the other social media sites as well.

As you will see while we go through this guidebook, there are actually a lot of different things that you are able to do when it comes to working with Google. You will get the benefit of different features, search engine help, SEO, and more. Utilizing all of these doesn't have to be expensive, and this is why working with Google is going to help you to really get a good return on investment with it.

Twitter

Twitter is a unique social media site that you can choose to use. Many businesses are turned off from it because there is a character limit on it, which can make it more of a challenge to get your message across. But this is not done because Twitter wants to make your life difficult or doesn't care about how hard this makes things. It is done because they want to encourage more conversations and relationships and interaction, rather than letting people put up really long and boring posts.

It is tricky to get onto Twitter and do some good posting, but if your research has shown you that this is where your customers are located, then this is a good place to start. It will allow you to focus on giving a message that is clear and concise, and providing your customers with something of value, rather than just rambling on.

Remember that this is more of a conversation rather than you just talking down to the other person. If you are able to share interesting links and pictures and more with your customer, talk back and forth with them, and really focus on the keywords and more that you want to use when it comes to working with Twitter, then it is going to be easier to stick out from the crowd and get the results that you would like at the same time.

YouTube

YouTube is a great option to go with, especially if you are a business that is creative, and really wants to show off some of your skills in a more visual way. Many companies that do more service oriented options are going to like this because it gives them a chance to show off their expertise on the subject, since they don't really have pictures of their products to sell. This doesn't mean that YouTube can't work for a lot of different businesses. Too many times a company is going to miss out on all of the great things that they an do on YouTube because they don't think it is for them, or they think that it is going to be too hard to work with.

YouTube is a great place to get ahead of the competition, and really show off what you are able to do. There are many options with YouTube that are going to be great, and showcasing your business through video and other graphics can really be different, especially if you are able to do it in a way that is creative and new.

When you go on YouTube, you need to take some time and really think through what you would like to do. It is not enough to just decide that you want to create a vide. There are millions of videos uploaded to YouTube and so many hours devoted to watching the content that is there. This can be a good thing because it allows you to really find the customers you want to work with, but it also means that you need to be able to stick out and impress the people on there.

If you make a video that is boring and won't get anyone past the first few minutes, if not even less, then you are going to run into some troubles. No one will watch, you won't get any more conversions or traffic to your site, and your sales will stay stagnant. Of course, you may find that the opposite is true if you are able to work on some really high quality videos over time. The more unique and creative and high quality your videos, the easier it is going to be for you to convert some of those customers you want.

LinkedIn

The final place that we are going to look when it comes to finding the perfect social media platform to grow your business is the LinkedIn platform. When you spend some time marketing on LinkedIn, it is going to help you to better engage with a community of professionals that will help to drive the actions that you think are the most relevant for your business.

There are a lot of businesses and young professionals who will spend their time on LinkedIn, looking for jobs, looking for a way to network with other similar professionals along the way, and more. If you have a product or serving that you are able to give to either side of the spectrum then this may be the place where you need to start.

LinkedIn, is not always the first place that people are going to consider when it is time to look for a place to advertise themselves. This is often seen as a way to find new employees, to find a new job, or to network in other ways that can grow the business. But your business is going to be able to do the same things, and get the same benefits, if you just learn how to use this social media site to your advantage.

There are some kinds of businesses that are going to do really well with this kind of platform. And then there are those who need to go and pick out a different platform to spend their time because they are never going to see results with this one. For example, if you are trying to sell ice cream in a small town up north, there probably isn't going to be a lot that you will get out of marketing on this site.

If you are a company that sells business attire, it may be a good to advertise on here. Since there are a lot of young professionals on this this, including ones who want to be able to get ready for an important interview and look their very best. If this or another similar product are available to you, then working with LinkedIn may be a great option.

As you can see, there are a wide variety of different types of social media platforms that you are able to use in order to help you to get the best results with your social media marketing. But with all the choices, it is easy to get caught up and just want to start advertising with everyone, with no attention to what you are doing or whether it is a good idea or not. Learning how to distinguish from all of the different social media sites and learning which ones are going to be the best for your needs is the biggest trick to learn.

Chapter 3: Facebook – The King of Social Media

The first social media site that we are going to take a look at is Facebook. Everyone has heard about Facebook, and it is likely that you have your own personal profile on this website. But it is now time to brig your business onto this media site and spend some time promoting yourself there in full force, if you really want to bring in the customers. Let's take a look at some of the ways that you are able to work with Facebook and get the best results possible.

Market with your Facebook Page

The first tool that you need to work with on Facebook, and one that doesn't cost you any money at all, is using a Facebook Page. This is similar to a personal profile, and it is the hub of information about your brand, whether you are offering a service, a product, or information for your company. Users are able to Follow or Like your page, which allows them to receive updates that you post on their news feed.

If you do this method, remind your customer to go through and actually click on the option to view posts first. Facebook has changed some things, and if customers do not do this part, they are not going to see these updates without going directly to your page. This is because Facebook wants you to pay for this kind of visibility and reach. If you can get customers to click on "See First" you will be able to reach them in a more organic manner, which can save you a lot of money.

You won't be able to get all of your customers to do this of course, and there is nothing wrong with using some paid advertising to get results on Facebook, but why spend more money than you need to when it comes to working with your marketing budget? When you ask people to come and like your Facebook Page, ask them to recommend that they follow and see your posts first. This can save you a lot of money from boosting each post, and will keep your customers coming back for more over time.

The trick is to find people who are going to be interested in liking your page. You want to make sure that you are reaching them as much as possible, but if you don't have many people who are interested in following you from the start, it takes some time to get off the ground. We will look at some ways that you are able to get more followers to your page later on, but first, let's explore some of the things that you can do to help set up a great Facebook Page so you can draw more organic traffic to the area.

How to set up your Page

As a business, you want to make sure that you are using your Facebook Page to its full potential. At the very least, you want to make sure that you are not using the Page in a manner that is going to drive away your customers and ruin your credibility and business. The good news is there are a few steps that you are able to follow that will help you to really get the most out of your page and see the results that you want from Facebook.

First, we need to take a look at choosing the right cover image and profile picture. If you have a logo, this is probably going to be the best thing to put as your profile picture. This helps to keep things simple, and ensures that others are going to be able to see what you have to offer and current and potential customers will know they are at the right place.

The cover image can be a bit different thought. You can have some fun with this one based on the kind of business that you are trying to run. It is really going to be up to you what you would like to do here and you can get creative if you would like. Sometimes adding contact information, pictures of your business or employees, or even some fancy artwork can help with this. Just make sure that it is professional, appropriate, and that it fits with the business that you are trying to run.

Next we need to focus on the about section. This is going to be placed right beneath that logo. This is a chance to really talk your business up, and to tell anyone who comes to your page more about you. You don't need to fit in every little thing about yourself here though. Just talk about some of the basics of what your company does. You can save some more of the details for the full about section later.

If you are in a hurry, you can use the About page of your blog of website, or some up with something unique to help you stand out to your customers. You want to work with a casual tone, one that is going to be friendly and informal for your customers.

The information that you post on your timeline, such as the status updates, need to have some purpose behind them. You want to make sure that the information has some use to your fans. Don't always have endless updates about the same thing, and don't try to post too often. Some ideas of what you can post to your audience would include:

1. Links to some articles related to your industry or your company.
2. Links to any posts that you add to your blog.
3. Coupon codes that are exclusive to your Facebook fans to help them save on your products.
4. Any announcements about new products.
5. Links to any kind of online tool that you think your fans are going to find the most useful.

No matter what you decide to post, make sure that it is useful to your customers. If it is just to fill up space, then it is not worth your time to post on here. Having a lot of variety of content, and finding the best time, and number of times, to post will make a world of difference in the results that you are able to get with this as well.

How do you know if you are posting at the right time, or if you are posting information that your followers will find useful? Check your statistics and some of the results that you get from them. Facebook Insights is a great tool that you can use that will offer you some great analytics for your page. You need to pay special attention to them to see if there are any times with a big surge from the fans, or times when the fans seem to go down. You can then start to see some of the patterns, and use this to your advantage.

Ways to drive traffic

The most obvious answer that you are going to see when it comes to this one is that you would use paid advertising on Facebook in order to bring in the customers. And you can certainly use this method if you would like. But our goal here is to get the most out of Facebook, without having to spend too much on our marketing campaign and spending for every little thing. Luckily, there are a few things that you are able to do in order to set up your Page and get more viewers without having to spend a lot.

First, consider adding information about your social media platforms on your website. If you already have a good amount of customers who visit your blog or your website and make purchases, let them know that you now have a Facebook Page. Let them know that they are going to find useful information, deals, and more on the page. There needs to be some incentive on the page to help get people to visit there and use your page. Adding some posts with special discounts that only your Facebook followers can get can be a great way to get them in to at least look.

If you are already on other social media platforms, then alert them that they can follow you on Facebook as well. You want to make sure when you are doing this that there is some incentive to make it happen though. If you are posting the same information and the same deals on each site, then there really isn't much of a reason for them to follow you on both.

Doing promotions and contests can be a great way to get people to follow you. If you can convince your current followers to get their friends and family to follow you as well, then you will be able to get more and more people on board. Offering some incentive to share your information to encourage them to get talk you up can be a great way to grow your business. You can offer a big discount, give them free products, and more can really help.

And of course, you need to make sure that your posts and information are always high quality. If you are just writing to fill up space, or your content is not done on a consistent basis, it is going to be almost impossible for you to get the results that you would like. Your customers want to find something of value, and they don't want to be an afterthought with you. Make sure that you are posting on a schedule that works for you that is consistent, and you are going to be able to form a good relationship with them.

Working with paid advertising on Facebook.

Now, you may notice that above we are talking about some of the things that you are able to do to organically reach your customers on Facebook. These are the things that you should do in order to start getting your customers in, and to save money. You can do quite a bit of marketing organically, even if you do use some targeted advertising, to save money and reach your fans in new and exciting ways.

With that said, Facebook is going to offer you a fantastic targeted advertising platform. You are able to create some ads that will be targeted to certain ages, locations, levels of education, and even the type of device that they are using when they search your site. Facebook also lets the users hide ads they don't like or a Like page button right below the advertisement.

Due to the fact that Facebook is able to gather a ton of demographic information concerning the users on it, it is going to have one of the best targeted advertising programs that you can find. You can basically choose anything that you want to base your targeting on, and you can even track how much success you will have with each of the segments.

While this has gotten them in a bit of trouble recently, we're just going to take a look at how this is going to benefit you as a marketer. You are able to choose to run your ads based on a per-click or a per-impression idea. Facebook is going to show you what bids are for ads that are similar to yours, so you have a better idea of your bid is going to be similar to what others are doing in the industry like you. You can also spend some time setting limits for each day so you don't blow your budget.

The advantage of using this is that ads on Facebook are really powerful, and you will notice that they are going to be more likely to succeed than groups or pages since you are the one who can choose who sees the ad. Of course, you do need to monitor what the costs of these are going to be to help you get the most out of the campaign, without spending too much money.

The first thing that we need to take a look at here is the type of ad that you want to run. There are a few types of ads that you can choose. These can include carousel, canvas, leads, offers, and even video. Each of them are going to have advantages over the other, and it really depends on what you want to do with the advertisement and even what you are trying to promote at the time. Some of the advertisement types that you can work with on Facebook includes:

1. Multi-product ads: These are often called carousel ads as well. With these, you are able to advertise more than one product ta a time. As a marketer it is a good way to check the engagement among some of the products that you are listing.

2. Domain ads: These are the types of ads that are going to contain one image and then there is a description that shows up at the top and a link to your website on the bottom. These are often known as page link ads. They are the

one that most advertisers are going to use on Facebook because they can be super effective.

3. Video ads: These are starting to really gain in popularity because it is a great way to influence various users you need to reach. While text can work well, videos are often much more effective at getting your message across, as long as you use them properly. They are often going to be used for retargeting and for increasing the awareness of your brand.

4. Offer ads: This is the type of ad where you give the viewer some information about an offer that you have. these are going to be targeted mainly to your current customers. you want to target them with this deal in order to get users to go directly to your website with a unique code to hopefully get them to purchase from you.

5. Canvas ads: These are a great option to work with because it is more interactive. You are able to look at the tab for publishing tools on your page. Then you can create the interactive part that you would like.

6. Lead Ads These are going to look the same as the standard Facebook ads, but they are going to be focused on getting the information about the user that you want, without having to

leave Facebook. You may be able to get some information like their name and their email address to use for more targeting later.

7. Branded content: These are going to be a type of sponsored ad. Often you are going to get together with another company or brand and then the two of you will post an ad together with a tag. Both of you can benefit from the exposure and the lower price for marketing.

8. Dynamic ads: And finally there are the dynamic ads. These are going to be able to collect some information from your website and then will make ads to your viewers based on that. You are able to add any personalization that you want to the ads. These are the kind of ads that show up when a customer has visited your site, and maybe left something in their cart that they didn't purchase yet.

Once you have an idea of what kind of ad you would like to run, you can go through and create a new ad campaign. You have to be the person who is running the page, so you need to be the administrator. From there, you can head over to the Ad Manager. It is a complicated tool simply because it has a lot of different features, but you just need to focus on a few of them to get started.

Powerful options for targeting

You will quickly find that Facebook is going to have some of the most powerful options when it comes to targeting your users. You are able to target pretty much everything that is on the profile of your user. You may start with location if that is the most important thing, and you get the option to specify by zip code, state, city, and more. This can be helpful if you are a local business. You can then mov eon to some of the demographics that are the most important to you such as their age, their education, where they work, their relationship status and more.

There are so many neat things that you are going to be able to do with this. For example, you may be able to do some targeting to figure out who has recently moved to the area. If you own a gym, for example, you could do some targeting and figure out who has just moved to that area and then make the advertisements for them.

You can target based on the interests the person has. This helps you to target towards people who may have interests that go for your business. You can target those who like a certain book if you would like, or target a private list of users if you have some email addresses that you have collected so far.

Customize your ads

And to finish this off, one of the biggest advantages that you are going to have to these targeted ads is that you are able to customize it and create the ads that work for a variety of demographic groups. Better-targeted ads are going to help you to get the best results.

For example, let's say you sell baseball equipment and you want to be able to target baseball fans. You may decide to create ads that are customized for different popular teams. You could create an ad that goes for Cubs fans, one that goes for Yankee fans, and one for Red Sox fans. Then you will have these specific ads shown to those who have already gone through and shown that they are interested in those teams.

There are so many things that you are going to be able to do when it comes to working with your marketing on Facebook. It is definitely a site that you need to spend some time on, but you do need to be careful. You want to make sure that you are using your budget as wisely and efficiently as possible. It is easy to spend a lot of money if you are not paying attention to what you are doing with your marketing. But if you pay attention and really learn how to leverage Facebook and do some of the organic work as well, you will be able to have an affordable and effective marketing campaign on Facebook.

Chapter 4: The Visual Effects of Instagram

It is definitely a good idea for your business to concentrate on working with the Instagram social media site. While Instagram may be younger, with fewer users, compared to the parent site of Facebook, but it is still a breakout social media site that you should spend some time on. You will be able to tell a visual story through a lot of different formats. And, if you are able to reach your target market in the proper manner, you will find that this can give you a huge return on investment compared to some of the other places you may choose to advertise.

Why would you want to work with Instagram? Because it is estimated to have 800 million active users each day. And it is likely that this amount is going to grow more and more throughout the years. People love the idea of being able to find the visual options that are on here, and it is a really unique way to showcase your business and your products.

This growth may be a little bit scary when you are first getting started, and you may be worried about some of the clutter that comes with it. Organically, you can make a start, but you may find that, like with your Facebook account, you are going to need to do a bit of paid advertising to help you stand out from the crowd. Let's look at some of the things that you are able to do in order to really get the most out of your marketing dollars and a great return on investment when you work with Instagram.

How to reach your audience organically on Instagram

The first thing that you need to focus on when it is time to bring in some of the great things that you can get out of Instagram will be reaching the audience in a more organic manner. This is going to help you to reach as many customers as you would like, without having to pay for paid advertising and wasting money on marketing.

While there is nothing wrong with working with paid advertising on Instagram, you do need to also work a bit on organically reaching your customers. And there are a few things that you are able to do to make this happen for you. Let's take a look at some of the best steps that you can take in order to really reach your target audience on Instagram.

There are a number of things that you are able to do to help organically grow your reach on Instagram and other sites along the way. Some of the techniques that are going to work well for most marketers, especially if you are using them the right way will include

Use the hash tags

While the image that you put up on your page is very important to the success of your Instagram campaign, hash tags are going to be one of the most important elements of your post. Captions can tell a story with the image, but the hash tag is going to get your image seen by those who may not be your current followers. When users on Instagram start to search for hashtags that are relevant in a specific industry, you want to make sure that your posts are one of the ones that show up. If they don't, then this means your competitors are there instead, and you are missing out.

There are going to be three main strategies that can be used for choosing hash tags. These include:

1. Use hash tags that are pretty popular, ones that have the best chance of getting search

for. This may end up with a lot of competition, but it still increases your chances of being seen.

2. Use some hash tags that are less popular, but still highly relevant to the work that you want to do. These may drive fewer users to your posts, but the ones who do find you based on these hash tags are going to be more targeted.

3. Use hash tags that are often thought to attract new followers. Some of the good ones to go with include #follow #follow4follow and #followme.

No matter which of the three strategies you choose to go with, or even if you decide to do a little combination of each one, try to use at least on hash tag on each post. Even more hash tags can be better because it increases the amount of reach you are able to get on this site.

Find the right amount of posts a day

The next ting that we need to take a look at is the idea of how many times you should post on your page a day. This is a question that is going to come with a lot of debate. Each marketer is going to come with a different answer to this one, and it is going to depend on your product, and your customer base.

There is a lot of information and advice that is conflicting when it comes to how often you will need to post on Instagram. In the long run, you are the one who needs to pay attention to the information that you are given, and the statistics that you look at, and then decide what seems to work the best for your needs. Some people may be fine posting just once a day, and others are going to need to post several times a day.

According to research that has been done on the idea of posting on Instagram, which was able to monitor 55 different brands who use Instagram, it was found that most brands would post somewhere in about 1.5 times on average a day. What seems to be more notable here is that posting more often didn't necessary result in less or more engagement. It all depends on what seems to work for your business, your time, and your customers.

In the past, most marketers were told to be overly careful about not posting too much on their pages. You shouldn't go too crazy with this and post fifty times a day every day. But if you want to post a few extra times one day, it is not going to hurt your engagement that much. You may need to experiment a bit and see how many postings a day will work the best for you.

Remember the vibe that comes with your brand

If you are looking around on Instagram, you will find that the brands that seem to have the most success there are the ones who will look carefully at their images and their posts and ensure that these are going to contribute to the identity of their brand. All of these companies are going to come with an overarching theme that ensures that all the videos, images, and other things stick with the same theme.

This is such a good thing and you need to stick with it in your own advertising as well. It is going to help your customers feel like they can really get to know you and our company. And when they feel that they are able to connect with you, they are going to stick around and see what more they are able to glean from you.

This means that you are going to have to carefully consider all of the pictures and videos that you want to put up on your Instagram business account. There are too many companies that will post things without thinking, and then it makes their brand look like a mess. While you don't want to have every picture become a clone of each other, it is a good idea to really think through any of the posts that you put up before you get started.

Steps to make sure your profile is optimized

It really doesn't take that long of a time for you to go through and properly optimize the profile that you are using on Instagram, but it can definitely make a big difference on how many people will actually click on your site. It can also make a difference on how they view your brand. Some of the tips that you can follow to help optimize your profile includes:

- Make sure that the description and the images on your profile go well with the vibe that you want to see in your company.
- Make sure there is always a link present that goes back to your website. You could even consider setting up a landing page that is specific for your visitors from Instagram, or you can make changes to the link to help promote a current campaign or other content.

- Use the logo for the company somewhere in the profile. This lets your users know that this profile is the official one for your company.
- Consider adding at least one brand specific hash tag to your profile. This makes it easier for your customers to know the profile belongs to you.
- If you are a local business, or have your own store, consider including your physical location into the profile as well.
- Make sure that if you have other social media profile that your images, and any other content, stay consistent throughout.

Growing your followers

If you do not take the time to grow up a good base of followers who are actively watching your posts and checking in with you on a regular basis, then all of the other things that you end up doing on this social media site are going to be worthless. The secret to growing your solid base properly is simple, but it does take some time and effort in order to see it happen.

The secret that we are going to follow on here is a natural engagement. When you naturally engage with your followers, you will find that they are more likely to stick around. What this means is that you need to respond to your customers, consistently post, keep the information engaging and prevalent to what you are doing, and more.

Now that we understand how this works, there are going to be a few different strategies that you are able to use in order to make sure this process works for you. Some of the strategies that can work when you want to grow your Instagram following include:

1. Remember that quality pictures and posts are always going to beat out quantity. If you have already started your account, make sure that you go through and edit it until only the very best is left. No one wants to follow you if all you have is thousands of pointless images that have nothing to do with your business.
2. Always have a good and relevant caption with your pictures. Asking a question within that caption can be a good way for you to increase your engagement.
3. Be consistent. Always remember who you are posting for, and remember why you are posting.

4. Use various tools like Piqura to see which images are leading you to the highest engagement, and then post more of them.

5. Engage on the photos that you most, and also on other profiles. As people start to see that you are interacting on a regular basis, they are going to start following you as well.

6. Make sure that if you are on Instagram, you should promote this account everywhere that you go. Promote it to other social media sites, on your physical marketing materials, and to your email subscribers.

The importance of being a follower

Unless you happen to be a big celebrity and go on Instagram, it is likely that you will have to do some work in order to get followers to pay attention to you and to even get people to follow you back in the first place. Not only should a business focus on following their followers back, but you need to take an active role in making and finding new people who will follow you.

This is sometimes hard. Just posting on your page is not going to be enough to bring in all of the people that you would like. You have to put in a little bit of legwork to see this happen. Some of the ways that you can work to find the right people you want to follow, an hopefully get them to follow you back will include:

1. Look around for the people you already know. When you are on your profile, head to the main page before clicking on the right hand corner of the top of the screen. From there you can tap on Find Friends and see who is on your suggested user list, contact list, and friend list.

2. Search for similar companies, or other companies you already know and who may have some followers who would like your company as well. You are able to find these using the search bar function.

3. Find others that you may want to spend your time following. Instagram makes this easy with their own Search and Explore feature. You just need to click on the magnifying glass icon and then do a bit of scrolling to figure out who is most recommended for you.

4. Follow influencers in the industry that you are already in. The program known as keyhole is going to help you search for users and posts using the hashtag from before, and then you

can go through all of the results looking at the number of likes found on the post.

5. Follow any of the users who are already following top influencers in your industry.
6. Search for hashtags that seem to go with your industry. This is a good way to help you do a bit of targeting on the users who are in your field or niche.
7. You can spend some time searching on Google as well. This helps you to find some of the most influential users in your industry.

Make sure your posts are engaging

One of the mistakes that you need to watch out for when you are working with Instagram is that you don't start to post the same type of content over and over again. Posting product shots and selfies may be something that you are used to working with, but it is also a good idea to mix up things a bit and then change the strategy. Try something new, or have a nice rotation of things that you would like to try along the way.

The neat thing with Instagram is that there are a lot of different options that you are able to choose from in order to help you mix up the content and to really make yourself stand out from the crowd. Some of the post ideas that you can try out to mix things up will include:

1. Photos that your users submit.
2. A day in the life shot that is going to show a bit of your personal life instead of just the business.
3. Holiday themed videos and images do well.
4. Some demos or tutorials that show the customer how to work with your product.
5. Simple image quotes on the picture or video. You are able to do this with the help of Canva.
6. Sneak peeks of any new product that is available for you to show your customers.
7. If you can, take some photos that are behind the scenes in your business to make the customer feel like they are getting information that others aren't.

Paid advertising on Instagram

Another option that you can work on is doing some paid advertising with Instagram. This allows you to reach for some of the customers who may not have been available for you in the past, and can even target your current customers to ensure that you are going to be able to make some of the sales that you would like to see.

When it comes to advertising with Instagram, there are a few different types of ads that you are able to work with. The most common types that you will want to spend your time on include:

1. Stories ads: These are the full-screen ads that will appear in between the stories of other users. This allows you to target your audience very specifically and makes it easier to reach a massive audience with that ad. You an add in filters, video effects, and even text to make the promotion more fun. And it is going to look and feel just like a normal post, allowing you to reach a bit audience without ruining the experience for the user. You can add in a call to action to get your audience to head back to your website or do another action that you want.

2. Photo ads: These are great for allowing a brand to really showcase their services and products with some compelling images. You can showcase some of your best products, and then add in a Shop Now call to action button before targeting who you would like the

pictures to go to. Just like with the stories, these are going to look just like the regular posts that you have, which can make the experience better for your audience.

3. Video ads: If you are able to make a good video that is short (fifteen seconds), then this may be the ad choice for you. This can be creative and can quickly make its rounds with a good call to action if you set it up in the proper manner.

4. Carousel ads: These ads are going to give the user a chance to swipe through a series of videos or images, and then there will be a nice call to action button that can lead the customer back to your website. These ads are going to do a few things such as sharing a multi-part story, showing more than one product, and even dive deep into one product or service with up to ten videos or images.

While you are able to advertise your Instagram posts on Facebook as well, we are going to keep this simple and look at how you can do paid advertising on your Instagram account. If you notice that you have a certain post or type of post that seems to get a lot of engagement and you want to grow this, you will be able to promote it within this app.

First, make sure that you have a business account set up (which you should at this point), and then you can go right to the post that you would like to promote. Click on the Promote button. It is likely that you will need to log in with your account from Facebook to authenticate who you are. Once that is done, you need to be able to select your goal.

There are a few goals that you can have including driving more people to your website, making more sales, or even maximizing the number of users who will see your post. You can also add in a call to action button of your choice, choose the audience that you want for the post (or you can let Instagram do this for you), and then choose the ad duration and the budget. When everything is set up for you the way that you want, hit Create Promotion and see how things go!

You can always make adjustments to the advertisements that you are doing, and you can learn from what you are doing along the way. if you notice that one type of demographic is really working for your needs, then go ahead and start relying on that a bit more. If you look at the statistics and see that something is definitely not working, then it is fine to drop that and move on. Advertising on Instagram or one of the other sites will be a big experiment in trial and error and it is fine to keep trying things until they work for you.

Chapter 5: Google and the Power of SEO

The next thing that you are able to take a look at when it comes to your options in social media and network marketing is on Google. Google is going to utilize the power of SEO to help those who are searching for you, or searching for topics related to your business and what you sell, to actually find you. Being able to do SEO on Google, and on a few other search engines, is going to be the best way for you to reach your customers where they are.

There are a lot of benefits of advertising and putting at least part of your marketing budget to Google. This is never more true than when you are a business just starting out. Think of it this way; there are more than 100 billion searches done on Google each month. And it is likely that some of those are going to be your potential customers. Doesn't it make sense for you to make sure that your customers are able to find you when they do these searches?

When you take the time to go through the steps that are needed to create a good campaign on Google, it is going to help you learn an important part of the marketing process, if you haven't done so already, and that is to determine who your ideal customer is, how to target them the best, and how to invest in the right steps to actually get these customers in the door (or to your website).

Marketing on Google is the first place you want to start. This is a way that you are able to directly advertise to those who are looking for your product and service. Usually when they are doing a search on Google or another search engine, they are at least looking for quotes and ideas, but many times they are ready to make their purchase if they find what they want. This is the perfect time to get ahold of your customers. If you show up and are relevant to the search they were done, then you may be able to convert them into paying customers.

You can also work with a feature that is known as Google AdWords. This is a method that marketers are able to use in order to reach out to their ideal customers and offer them your business as an answer to what they are looking for when they search online. This can be a good way to moderate your costs because there is no minimum ad buy on it. As a smaller business, this may be a good place to start because it can save your budget and help you get your business up and running.

Organic advertising on Google

The first thing that we need to look at is some of the organic ways that you are able to grow on Google. Setting up some of these are going to help you to do a lot better when it is time to bring in some of the paid services that you want to use with Google. Keep in mind with this one, you are going to be able to use a lot of the tools with Google for free. For example, you can look through different keywords with Google AdWords or Google Keyword Planner in order to figure out which keywords will be able to help you set up your blogs and websites the proper manner.

When you are ready to work with organic reach on Google, you need to concentrate on your website, and maybe even consider a blog. You will be able to take a look at some of your products and figure out if there is a common string that you are able to stick with between all of the products. Then see if you are able to start a blog that will link back to your website.

You can then start to post a few well-done articles and blog posts on a regular basis to help you to reach your customers. For example, if you sell fitness equipment, you may want to write articles about the best time to workout, the different types of working out, the benefits of working out, proper nutrition, and more. These will help you to see the results that you want overall, and will make it easier to add in the right phrases and keywords to your website so that you can rank on SEO.

SEO is going to be more effective when you do some of the paid advertising options that are available through Google. But if you already have this set up well on your blog or website, and the works are done in the right manner (meaning that they are placed throughout nicely and the article is actually going to be valuable to the customer), then when you start to implement paid advertising with Google, things are really going to take off.

The different ways to advertise on Google

There are a lot of options that you can use when it is time to advertise on Google. Each marketer is going to have to look at the options and decide which of the options seems to be the best for them. Some marketers may find that working with AdWords and just using paid ads is going to be enough for them. Others may want to use some of the other tools that are available through Google and will include tools like YouTube, organic search marketing, Google Shopping, Google Plus, and Google Maps to name a few. These take a bit more effort, but can ensure that you are able to find the customers that you need.

You will find that using several of the assets from Google in your campaign can really help you to get more out of your efforts, and will allow you to make adjustments to your strategy over time. These adjustments can be made based on what you see is working through the analytics and tools that are offered. There are a lot of options that you can choose to make sure that your business is optimized as much as possible through Google, and some of the top options to work with will include:

1. Google Play
2. Google News
3. Google My Business
4. Google +
5. Google Maps
6. YouTube
7. Google Search

You will find that working with the keyword planners and analytic tools are going to be another part that you need to focus on with advertising.

These are so important because they help the marketer get the insight that they need to ensure they are always making the right choices each time. When you work with the Google Keyword Planner for example, you will be able to look up words you would like to rank in SEO and figure out the bids you should pay, whether they are good keywords or not, and more. These help you make sound decisions based on your business and what has been working for others in the industry.

Using the AdWords platform in Google

Although you do get some examples when it comes to working with Google in any marketing strategies, one of the easiest ways for beginners to start with this is setting up your AdWords account.

AdWords is going to be an advertising platform that Google offers to businesses to run ads on the search results page. With this option, a user or a marketer is able to spend some time researching phrases or individual terms, and then using them in their website to get themselves on results page. If you use this platform, there is also going to be an "ad" mark on your search result. When you use this kind of service, you are going to be able to bid on some of the keywords that you think your potential customers will type into the search bar when they are looking for your service or your product.

This can be important for you to grow your business. Depending on the keywords that you decide to use, it can get a bit expensive. But it does ensure that you are going to show up at the top of the search results when a potential customer is looking for your products or services. Since many customers do not want to search all day, they are likely to at least click on the first result they get, even if it is an ad. And if you actually picked out good search terms to use, and you are careful with creating a high quality website that your customers will enjoy, then you will be more likely to make the sale in the process!

This brings up another key point. Google is not going to just let anyone with a website do this and rank high for all the keywords they want. Google wants people to keep coming back and using them. So they do have a few guidelines and rules that you are going to have to follow. They are going to look through your website and check out the quality and the relevance of your account to determine whether your website can be ranked with certain keywords.

Google + Page for Business

In addition to working with the paid advertising that we just talked about, marketers are going to have the option to work with a feature from Google known as Google +. This is a kind of tool for social media that will make it easier for you to reach out directly to the customers you have.

Like with some of the other social media sites that we have talked about in this guidebook, Google Plus is a way for you to communicate and interact in a more direct manner with your customers while still making sure that the context of your brand and business are provided. Google + can also have a big impact on your search traffic volume and SEO compared to some of the other sites of social media, simply for the fact that it is connected to Google and some of the other options they provide.

If you go through and create your own business page with the help of Google My Business, you will find that you become a featured business in search results any time that a user is looking for local businesses. This puts you right at the top of the search engines, and can make it easier for the right potential customer to find you when they need you the most.

When you decide to set up this kind of business page using the tools that Google provides, you will automatically be setting up your own Google + page as well. When you are able to put both of these tools together, it is going to make it easier for your search results to go up. Plus, this page provides you with a social media presence so that you can easily communicate with your customers, answer questions, share important information, and really get out there and represent your brand.

Can I work with Google Maps in my marketing?

Any time that you set up your business page here, you can also use the feature that is known as Google Maps. This is useful to ensure that you show up, along with your location, any time that a potential customer searches for keywords that relate back to you. People who are looking for some of the local businesses that may be able to provide them with a certain service or product will be able to type in the keywords that they want before seeing your location on the map feature as well. This comes with your website or Google Plus page link, as long as you have done the right work and are ranked high enough to be in these results.

If you spend the time updating this Business page with information that is accurate and complete, this can help your rankings. Google will be better able to match your business with the searches that relate to it. Some of the things that you need to do to make this happen is add in the physical address, phone number, category of the business, and then verify the location, and you will be placed on Google Maps. The more detailed information that you are able to add about this, the easier it will be for you to show up in the right search engines, and for your potential customers to find you.

What is Google product listing ads

If you are working with a business that is going to sell some physical products rather than just working with a service, then you are able to work with the feature known as Google Shopping. This is a tool in marketing that will help you to increase your traffic quite a bit while also making sure that your revenues are going to see a boost.

Google Shopping is great because it will allow your users see your product show up in a product listing ad that includes the image of one of your products, the name of your store, sometimes reviews, and the price. Try this out real quick. Type in some kind of item that you want to purchase, such as a new Fitbit. When you type this into Google, there are often some images with prices and company names that show up right along the top. This is because of Google Product listing ads. And if you decide to add this to your marketing campaign, your products could end up on the top of search results as well.

Google Shopping is going to be managed within AdWords, but you are able to set up a bid on your products, rather than specific keywords for a traditional text ad. Google is able to help you out here to ensure that you are choosing the keywords that are right for your products. This ensures that you are going to appear at the top whenever users type those words into the search results.

Product listing ads are a great thing to consider because they will ensure that you are going to get some more clicks from new potential customers, especially ones who aren't already familiar with your company and can become new customers. You will find that Google Shopping has really grown to become more popular as its comparison shopping revenue is going to keep on increasing, making it a very effective tool that you can add to your marketing plan.

Other Google Aps for advertising

For companies who are just getting started with the idea of cloud computing, you may want to work with Google Apps for Business, or G Suite, to help. This can streamline the whole process and ensures that you are able to keep everyone on the same page together all of the time. For G Suite, there are actually a few options available to you depending on your budget and how much you need to get done. For example, the lower end that allows you to just do the basics is going to be about $5 a month for each user.

There are a lot of different things that you are able to do with G Suite, so it may be worth your time to check it out. With this feature, you are able to verify the website for your business, and even set up your own email, one that all your employees are able to use, that includes your domain name. Think of the level of professionalism you are able to add if you have a business with its own email address. This can also help customers know who you are any time they read your emails or need to communicate with you.

This feature is also going to make your work and marketing a lot easier, especially when you are on the go. It can help you with email, shared calendars, and Google Drive. If you and your team are on the go quite a bit, these can help you to communicate and share information when it is needed. Using these business apps can speed up the process and ensures that you are as efficient as possible.

Working with the Analytics

Before we end our discussion on advertising with Google, we need to take a moment to explore some of the analytics that you are able to do with this site. You are going to end up wasting a lot of time, money, and resources if you just randomly use the features and have no idea what is working or not. Google Analytics can help with this because it can give you a ton of important statistics about your website while also providing you with the feedback that you need to know how the campaign is really working.

When you have started a campaign and let it go for a bit, you will be able to log into your profile and see how many visitors are heading to your website, where the visitors are located, where all of this traffic is coming from (is it through SEO, your blog, from other social media and so on), which tactics in marketing seem to be working the best, and how many of the visitors who come to your site are then converting into paying customers? You can even split it up and see how many customers or visitors are from PC's and how many are mobile users.

It is definitely worth your time to spend your efforts looking at the analytics on occasion and making any adjustments that are needed. You can use these analytics in order to track different aspects of your marketing campaign and see which ones seem to have the biggest impact when it comes to traffic to your website and highest conversion rates.

As a marketer, you may also use some of the other tools that are out there, such as Keyword Planner and Google Trends, to help you figure out the right keywords to use in various campaigns base don how many customers are using them and how well they are trending. You can then take those keywords and use them either in your organic search strategy, or in your AdWords campaign.

Keeping a close eye on your campaigns and learning what is working best and what you should avoid can be so important when it comes to helping you get the results that you want out of Google. Google has a ton of features that will help you to grow your business and will ensure that you can reach the customers that you want. It doesn't just rely on one platform, but a bunch of features that get the job done. And learning how to use it along with other social media options is going to make a difference in how fast your business is able to grow.

When you are looking around to see which social media sites you would like to use in order to make sure your business is going to really grow, you need to make sure that you add at least a bit of Google marketing to the mix. When this is added in, you are going to see some amazing results that will ensure your business is going to reach the new heights that you would like.

Chapter 6: The World of Twitter

The next social media site that we are going to look at is Twitter. With more than 313 million active users each month, and a demographic that is young too, Twitter can be a great place for you to market yourself and see some great results. And you will find that it is pretty easy to set up your own Twitter profit. You just need to come up with your own handle (the name of your profile), upload a good picture to be your profile picture, fill outa bio, and send out the first Tweet and you are ready to go. There are more steps to growing the account, but these simple steps will at least help you to get yourself started.

Growing a real following through Twitter can take some more work than just sending out Tweets when you have a big event or a new product. Twitter is useful because it helps you to engage with your audience and actually interact with them. This isn't going to happen if you just send out a few Tweets a year. Let's take a closer look at Twitter and how it can help you grow your business.

How is Twitter different from the rest?

The approach that you have to each social media site that you work with should be a bit difference. You won't be able to use the same strategy that you do with Twitter as you do with your Facebook marketing plan. It is important that you learn more about the way Twitter works and the best way to use it in order to get the best benefits.

There are many different ways that a business is able to utilize Twitter in order to reach their needs. Some of the main ways include:

- Managing their reputation
- Branding themselves
- Networking so they an find other similar businesses and potential customers in the industry
- Interacting with their customers, and potential customers.
- Driving engagement for some of the promotional activities that they are working on
- Sharing the content and information that they have about their business and about their products.

Just like with all of the other social media sites that we have talked about, most of these activities are going to have to do with interactions. It is not just about broadcasting out your content, like what can happen with Pinterest and Instagram sometimes. Twitter works because of open communication.

Now that we know a bit about the importance of Twitter and how businesses will often use it, it is time to go into some of the things that you need to know in order to get started with marketing on Twitter. We are going to go beyond the how to for setting up a good profile. We are going to look at some of the real strategies that will ensure you are able to reach your customers and that you won't waste your time through this platform.

What is Twitter Chats and how can I use it?

Many of those who are interested in working with Twitter are curious about the way they can gain followers While followers are important, you want to make sure that you have followers who are active rather than ones who just click on you and then never look at you again. The answer to this kind of problem on Twitter is going to be Twitter chats.

These are a feature of Twitter that have been around for some time, but there are a lot of marketers who are slow to trying them out and learning the power that comes with them. But as a new marketer on Twitter, you need to pay attention to these chats and see what they are able to do for you.

One of the main reasons that these chats are going to be so effective for you to use is because the ones who are on them are active followers on Twitter. Those on this feature are on Twitter and purposely there to interact, learn more, and try new things. These are the best followers because they are the ones who will talk back to you, reply to any of the Tweets that you put up, will Retweet your content and messages, and can even help you to get things started.

Now, there are going to be a variety of Twitter chat groups, so make sure that you do some research and find the ones that are specific to your personal industry. This will help you to really get the results that you want and will ensure that you will talk to others who are interested in your content and what you have to say. And remember, you can't just post an ad and run away. You need to be present, asking and answering questions, interacting, and finding ways to really add value for others who are already there.

Twitter video

While Twitter is not always the first option that people are going to think about when they want to get started with video marketing, this is still something that you can consider adding into your Twitter marketing campaign. Twitter may not be as advanced with video marketing as you will see with YouTube, but it does give you a few options that can be helpful when you want to promote using videos on this site.

The first option is to use the native video feature that is already available through Twitter. This feature is going to allow you to record videos that are up to 140 seconds long. When these videos are done, you are able to upload these straight to the stream on your Twitter profile. If you want to make things easier and your videos is going to be about two minutes or less, then this option can be a great one to choose. If you would like to do something a bit longer, or you would like some more features to use, then you may want to go with the second option.

Another option that you can go with when you use Twitter is Periscope. This is a live streaming app that Twitter actually owns. Periscope is able to integrate your content into Twitter, which means that if you do a live stream, this is going to show up on the Twitter feeds for your followers. Then, when the stream is over, that recording will still sit around so your viewers can watch it whenever is the most convenient for them.

The second option can be nice because you get the chance of going live. This attracts more attention from your potential customers because they can watch you, ask you questions, and so much more. Add in the fact that these Live videos were able to get more than 31 million views in 2016, and more as time has gone on, it is definitely worth your time to add at least a few of these videos onto your Twitter feed on occasion.

Paid advertising with the help of Twitter

There are a lot of different options that you can choose from when it comes to a Twitter ads. Some of the best options that you can choose from include:

Promoted Tweets

These types of tweets are simply tweets that you are going to pay to get displayed to people on Twitter who are not already following you. They can work just like regular Tweets in that others can comment on them, like them, and even Retweet them as they like. They will also look like regular Tweets in many cases, other than they will have a Promoted label on them.

These Tweets are going to appear on the users' timeline, or on their profile, near the top of search results, and even on the desktop and mobile apps for Twitter. This is a great way to discuss your brand and let new potential followers know more about you. If you are careful with the way that you set these up, and you make them really informative and valuable, it is likely that you will get a ton of interactions. The more interactions, the more people who will see the advertisement, and the easier it will be for you to get new followers.

Promoted accounts

Another option that you can work with is a promoted account. These are sometimes known as

Followers campaign. Hey will make it easier for you to promote the account you are using for business to targeted users who aren't following you yet, but who may find some of your content interesting. This can be a great way to find people who are already interested in topics in your industry so they are more likely to start following you.

These accounts will show up on the timelines of those people you follow. They can also show up in the Who to Follow suggestions and search results. They will list out that they have been promoted, but they will also have a Follow button on them so your potential customers have a chance to click and start following your page.

Promoted trends

When you are taking a look at a topic on Twitter and you notice that it is trending, this means that there are a lot of people on the social media site who are talking about this kind of subject. This is also a hot topic that Twitter is sure to place on the timeline of many of their users, on the Twitter app, and on the Explore tab. If you are able to do a promoted trend, you can promote the hashtag of your choice and get this in the same place to increase your visibility overall.

Any time that one or more of the users on Twitter decide to click on the trend that you are promoting, they are going to be able to see an organic list of search results that have that have that specific tag in them as well. What shows up differently here, and is going to benefit you the most, is that with a Promoted Tweet, your business is going to be the first option that shows up on this list.

So, people will start to see this hashtag and may use it for some of the posts that they do as well. This helps you to gain a bit more organic exposure, and it is likely that people are going to see your business as the top result because of your promotion. This ensures that you are able to get the most reach possible for your campaign.

Working with the automated ads

And the final promotional method that you are able to use when you go on Twitter is to work with an automated ad. Twitter has a neat thing that is known as the Twitter Promote Mode, and it works really nicely for those who are not familiar or all that comfortable with marketing on social media yet, and who would like a bit of help.

If you go with this option, it will be around $99 a month to use it. When it is turned on, the first ten Tweets that are done in the day will be promoted automatically to the audience that you have selected, as long as they are a high quality target audience as determined by Twitter. Replies, Retweets, and quote Tweets will not be included in this. You will also be able to work with a campaign for a Promoted Account that is ongoing at all times.

Remember that if you do go with this one, you may have to go into it and make the necessary adjustments as needed. For example, you will need to take the time to write out the Tweets that should be used, you need to decide on the right audience for the ads to target, and more. However, if you are able to do this, it is estimated that this feature from Twitter will help you reach an additional 30,000 people and gain at least 30 new followers to your business, so it could be worth your time.

As you can see, there are a number of different benefits that come with working on Twitter. Twitter is a great way for you to promote your business and open up communication with your customers in a way that just isn't found with other sites. Rather than just posting information (although you are able to do this on occasion), you will spend time in conversations with your customers, interacting with them, and more. Twitter can be a great idea to implement into your marketing campaign to get the most out of reaching your customers.

Chapter 7: Can My Business Benefit From YouTube?

The next thing that we are going to take a look at is how you can use YouTube to help promote your business. This is not a traditional site that a lot of companies will look at. If they aren't into advertising or something creative like that, they assume that they are not going to be able to see any results if they chose to go with marketing on YouTube.

The truth is, anyone is able to see their business grow if they just learn how to use YouTube in the proper manner. There are a lot of different things that you can do in some of your videos, and sometimes it is just a matter of thinking about what your customers want, or even just thinking outside the box and seeing what you are able to come up with. Let's take a look at some of the things that you can do with your videos on YouTube, and how you can increase your reach, both organically and through paid advertising, on YouTube, no matter what kind of business you are.

Optimized videos to get more searches and clicks

It isn't a big secret. If you want to make sure that you are able to see some success on YouTube, then you need to make sure that your videos are all optimized to work well not only on YouTube, but also on Google. By adding in the right keyword sin the right places, such as in your descriptions, tags, and titles, you can make it so much easier for customers to find you when they do a search.

We need to start by looking at the title. According to Google, it is recommended that you use the keyword you want to focus on first, then the branding second. This helps it to be more friendly in an SEO sense. You could also add in a season and episode number, if you find that is relevant, but put these right at the end. Your goal with this title is to create a clear picture so the customer knows what they are going to see when they click there, while also maintaining your SEO so you are easier to find. Try to keep the title short and sweet and to the point as well.

Working with tags is another thing to consider here as well. These tags are pretty simple and they are just going to be the main keywords that are going to relate to that video you are creating, and will tell others what your video is all about. For the most part, it is believed that YouTube is going to concentrate mostly on the first few tags that you write out, so try to make those ones as good as possible, or have your most important keywords close to the front. Your aim is to use all of the 120 characters you are given, but make sure they are all relevant to your video for the best results.

The description is going to be next. You need to spend time on this one to ensure it is high quality and will garner the attention that you want. Include a call to action so the viewers know what you would like them to do when they are done watching the video. It can be something like asking them to visit your website or to watch one of your other videos depending on your goal. Remember that the first few sentences of this description are going to show up in search results, both on Google and YouTube, so make sure that you put a lot of value there.

There needs to be a thumbnail that comes with the video as well. This is the image that the user is going to see that comes with your video. Don't skimp on this; try to bring in a high quality one that is going to draw in your customer and will help them to choose your video over one of the others that are available. You want to do an image that is 1280 X 720 pixels.

YouTube can also generate a thumbnail as well, or you an upload your own.

How to promote your videos as well as your YouTube channel

The next thing we need to look at when it comes to organic reach with your videos is the different methods of how you can promote your videos and your channels. There are three main ways to get more views for the videos that you are creating and adding to your channel. These three ways will include:

1. Getting a rank that is higher for YouTube or Google keyword searches.
2. Having a subscriber base on YouTube that is large
3. Promoting your channel and your videos through other web properties.

The previous section already took some time to discuss the best ways to optimize the videos that you are working on. Growing your channel on YouTube, and being able to promote these channels and videos on other web properties that you own will be the next, and sometimes the most challenging part, of this whole process. Some of the ways that you can help increase your views and subscribers to your videos includes:

1. Promote these videos and your YouTube channel on the other social media profiles. You should include some hash tags that are relevant on these posts so that you get even more reach.

2. Engage with your loyal fans. When you spend time looking through the Creator Dashboard, you will see which users are the most engage with the content you provide. You can consider involving these fans in some way to nurture some brand ambassador relationships later on.

3. Add a widget for YouTube on your blog: You can use a tool such as Tint to help you display a number of videos, these can be your own or someone else's, in a widget that goes right on your blog or website.

4. Collaborate with other business owners who run a complimentary niche: approach some other YouTubers and see if they are willing to promote your videos if you promote theirs. You can even consider co-branding videos in order to use them for both audiences.

5. Engage with your users, both on their videos and on yours: Social media is going to see the best results when you interact and engage with others users, but this doesn't mean that you should just stay on your own channel. Leave comments that are well thought out on videos and respond to any comments left on yours. Remember, the more interactions you have with your videos, the higher you will rank in the search.

6. Share your videos on your email list: Direct the audience to your embedded videos on your site in order to increase your page views and your video views.

7. Embed the videos onto your blog or website: Add videos to existing posts on your blog, or you can even come up with new blog posts that are specifically there to promote your videos. This will help you to increase your video views, and increase your pageviews on the site.

Making your reach organic on YouTube can take some time and may not happen as quickly as you would like. But it is a great way to ensure that you are finding people who are truly interested in the content that you try to provide. There are also some paid options that you can choose to work with as well, but whether these are going to be as successful as the organic reach that we have just talked about, depends on your audience, on the products that you are trying to sell, and more.

Paid advertising on YouTube

You also have the option of doing paid advertising on YouTube to help you reach more potential customers. Plus, paid advertising is often going to be much faster than what you are able to do on your own organically. On the YouTube platform, you are able to turn any video that is already on your page into an ad, or you can create a video that you want to use specifically as an ad. With the right targeting of keywords, you can make sure that your video is one of the first ones that shows up in search results, and that it appears alongside other similar videos when your potential viewer is online.

Marketers on YouTube are going to have a few options that they can use when it comes to targeting and setting up their YouTube ads. You can target based on a variety of demographic factors like keywords, gender, age, location, and so on. You can even choose how big the ad is going to be. Many marketers like to go with the larger ads that are 850 by 250, though there are other options that you may want to experiment with a bit to see if they work for you.

If you want to make sure that your videos are getting a boost each time you put them online, or you want to really grow your following and your profits online, then advertising on YouTube is one of the best options for you. For a marketer who has never worked online or with YouTube, the options may seem overwhelming, but it is a great way for you to get more social reach and can help you to get off the ground.

There are a lot of marketing options that are available when you decide to work with YouTube, especially when you are doing paid advertising. YouTube ads are the most common ones that you are going to use. And these will just be a video of your choice. Of course, you should never just randomly put a video up. You need to go with one that is high quality, one that you think may go viral if possible (this is a hard thing to predict, but if you aim for a good video that is catchy, it could happen), and one that may get the viewers to head over to your channel to see what other videos they are able to purchase.

If you are able to make a good video, one that has a good hook in the beginning that will keep customers on the video rather than clicking away, you are going to increase the reach that you have online. This is going to help you get the results that you would like, and will ensure that your return on investment from running these ads is as high as possible.

What is TrueView

One neat feature that you are able to explore when it comes to advertising on YouTube is the idea of TrueView. This is something that you are likely to hear about pretty early on when you start marketing. This feature is basically a way that YouTube is able to create some commercials, commercials that look similar to the ones that you may see with other online television or streaming services. This is actually going to be a highly successful form of advertising with YouTube and one that you as a business should take full advantage of.

When you are looking into doing a TrueView ad, you will basically need to start out by creating a short video for something that you want to advertise for, whether it is your channel, your brand, a product, or something else. Your goal here in most cases is to get any potential customer who sees the ad to really learn some more about the company.

Then YouTube will take these videos and place them at the beginning of another video that is being monetized. There are a lot of individuals and even companies out there who post videos and then earn money when advertisers put their videos at the front, and sometimes in the middle, of those videos. This helps those individuals to make money online, and ensures that you are able to gain more viewers.

Now, for this to work, the video that you would like to post to needs to be monetized. This is why there are still some videos that show up on YouTube that have no commercials on them. If the poster doesn't monetize their videos, it means that they are not going to have any commercials show up, and they are also not going to earn any money from advertisers on the videos as well. This can help direct your search when it is time to figure out which videos you would like to post on or not.

TrueView is not the only way that you can work to advertise your company on YouTube though either.

Another option is to work with InDisplay Ads. These kind of ads are going to show up as a thumbnail next to the video that a viewer is looking at during that time. sometimes these are going to look similar to the PPC ads that other social media sites will use, but they will also come with a little thumbnail of the business or the video as well. From here, the viewers are able to choose if they would like to click on these ads. These are a great option if you would like to be able to promote other videos that may be present on your channel at this time. These InDisplay ads are a good way to restart a campaign that is viral or to get started with having people watch a bunch of your videos at once.

There are a lot of different options that you can utilize when it comes to TrueView, and you can be a bit creative in order to stand out from the crowd. You will notice though that when you use some of these TrueView ads, you are not going to be billed in the same manner that you are for a regular AdWords ad that you would place with Google.

InStream ads are going to be billed on a cost per view format. This means that you are going to be charged any time that someone clicks on your ad and then stays there for a minimum of 30 seconds. If this happens, regardless of the conversion or not, then you will have to pay. If the viewer doesn't click on the ad, or they don't stay for the 30 seconds, then you won't have to pay for that.

Now, you really need to make sure that you are creating videos that are high quality and will keep the interest of your viewer until they get to the call to action and perform the action that you would like. YouTube ads are not stuck. This means that your viewers are able to skip them after three seconds, both on a PC and their mobile device. If the video doesn't hold their interest, they are going to be able to skip past you without getting much of a chance to know much about you.

This does allow you to get yourself in front of other people more, and some viewers, if you made the video well and had a nice hook in the beginning, may remember you and head to your channel to check out more as well. But it means that the standards are high. If you just assume that any old videos is going to do the trick and you don't come up with something that is high quality and attention grabbing, then you are going to end up with a lot of people just skipping over the ads that you are creating.

The ads that we have talked about here are going to fall into the cost per view format so keep that in mind. What this means is that you are going to be charged any time that one of your potential customers clicks on the thumbnail of the video and watches it on their page. If the customer sees the add, and then doesn't actually click on it, then you won't be charged at that point. But any time a customer clicks, even if they don't end up finishing the video, you will be charged for that.

The above is the two main options that you are going to have when it is time to work with the option of paid advertising on YouTube. Having a good plan, and understanding how each works and whether they are going to be the best for you is so important when you are trying to set up a campaign that works for your needs. But the number one thing that you need to do, no matter if you are working on your organic reach or paid advertising, is the quality of your video.

People are not automatically going to see your business and then click on the link to make a purchase. You need to give them something to incentivize them to go there, a good video can be a good start. Show them about your company. Show them what you are able to offer. Or find something else that you are able to put into your videos to really impress them and convince them that it is worth their time to check you out. without this catchy video, and without any enticement to at least head over to your website, marketing on YouTube is going to be worthless for you.

Chapter 8: Finishing Out with LinkedIn

The final social media site that we are going to spend some time on now is LinkedIn. This is not a traditional social media site that you may consider. Known as being a place for young professionals to meet, and maybe even find their first job out of college, it seems like it may not be the best place to find those who would want to purchase your products. However, if you are able to use LinkedIn correctly, and you have the right kind of products or services, it can be a really successful way for you to earn an income and increase your revenues and sales in no time.

LinkedIn is going to be a great way for you to promote your own business. In fact, there are a lot of different benefits of using this and some of the top ones that will affect your business (and why you should consider marketing on this social media site) will include:

1. It is estimated that there are at least 65 million business professionals on this site. These professionals are not only from the United States, but from the whole world.

2. The average member on LinkedIn has an average annual household income of $109,000. This is way above the average for most families, meaning that they have some disposable income, for the right products.
3. It is estimated that one person is going to create a LinkedIn login every second. This means that your market is going to grow over time, helping you to reach more and more people too.
4. Nearly half of the members on LinkedIn are going to have the authority to make decisions for their companies. If you are able to interact with them and reach them at the right times, that could be very beneficial for you.

If your business is looking to grow through mentorship, referrals, and networking, then it is easy to see why you would want to spend some time on LinkedIn. Like some of the other forms of marketing online that we have taken a look at, marketing a small business is going to be inexpensive on LinkedIn (you can even set up the profile for free), and it is extremely effective.

How to get started with the marketing

Now that we have an idea of the benefits of LinkedIn and some of the reasons why your business would benefit from using it, it is time for use to learn some of the steps that you are able to work on in order to see the most success with LinkedIn.

The first steps that you need to work on to see the most results with LinkedIn is to make sure that you create your own login, if you aren't already one of the members on there. you should also spend some time on the profile. You want to use the right keywords and the right information in order to make sure that others know how your business is able to help them. Your goal here is to make sure your profile pops out and can attract more customers to you.

Unless you are working your business as a freelancer, then it may be a good idea to create a company page on LinkedIn for the business. You will be able to set up that profile as a new business page as you work on the resume part of your profile. Your company page can then be linked in from the resume that you put on your profile. With these basics for your LinkedIn profile in place, you can start to market your business to others who are on this social media site.

Advertising on LinkedIn

There are going to be two ways that you can decide to dive into promotions and advertising on LinkedIn. You can choose to go with either the proactive action or the passive approach. No matter which approach you decide to go with, the more time and the more effort that you decide to put into your marketing efforts on this social media site, the bigger the rewards are going to be.

So, first we are going to take a look at some of the things that you would like to do with passive marketing on LinkedIn. Simply creating your own profile, working on some connections, and ensuring that you keep your account updated could be enough to help you get the attention of partners, influencers, customers, and clients you would like to work with.

This sometimes seems too easy to be true. But it can actually provide you with a number of benefits in the process. Some of the benefits that you are going to be able to get by doing the passive marketing method is going to include:

1. Helps you to gain some exposure to people who are looking for your services or products.

The search feature on this site will allow others users to find you when they are looking for the products and services that you offer.

2. Getting you to find potential customers. Your business connections on this site are going to help you get "in" with the businesses and people you need, many of whom you may not be able to reach in other methods.

3. Displaying your recommendations when others give them on the site. Recommendations are basically word of mouth testimonials for your business and for you. They are going to prove how credible you are and they will encourage people to do business with you.

The next thing that you need to focus on here is going to be the more proactive marketing techniques. Like most of the other tactics that you are able to use when on this site, the more active you are, the faster and more effective the results are going to be. There are a few steps that you are able to work with to bring in more customers as well.

First, make sure that you are posting updates on a regular basis. Make sure that your customers are up to date on what you want to work with and what you are going to do in the future. Include updates that are going to be of the most interest for potential customers and clients. Focus on how what you are doing will be able to help your customers achieve their goals.

Next, spend some time participating in groups. You want to pick the right groups though. Pick out ones that are going to be within your own interest and business. Discussion participation is going to get others to see you as an expert in your field. Of course, don't go on thee groups and then start to spam others all of the time. Make sure that you are there adding in value. Answer questions of your customers, do posts that are going to add value, and only add in your business when it is there.

While you are on this site, make sure to send out invitations and messages to those who are in your network, as well as to those who are in the groups that you belong. Again, you don't want to become a spammer or pester others. Your goal is to create the right connections, and the best way to do this is to make it beneficial to the other person and to you.

As you are doing all of this, you want to make sure that you look into some of the options that come with advertising and an upgraded, paid membership on this site. This is going to give you some more benefits that will help you to grow your business more, and more contact options as well. And advertising on LinkedIn is still seen as a great bargain while still growing your business quickly.

Creating a LinkedIn Ad campaign

Now that we have looked at some of the different things that you are able to do with your account, it is time to learn how to create your own ad campaign. To get started with this kind of campaign, you will need to have a few things including a video if you would like, some ad copy, a good understanding of the audience that you want to work with, and your own profile.

Once you are ready, you need to go to your login page and the LinkedIn Ads part. Then click on Get Started. You will then be able to see two different types of options for the campaigns that you are able to run including Create an ad, and Sponsor an Update. We are going to take a look at doing the ad, but if you think the other kind will help, you can do that one as well.

So, first we need to take a look at creating your ad. There are going to be a few different areas that you need to fill in before you are able to make this work well for your needs. Some of the information that you should fill out to get the most out of your ads will include:

1. Campaign name. You need to come up with a name that you would like to come up with for your campaign. This can keep things organized and makes it easier to find the information that you need.
2. Ad language; You are able to choose from a few options when it comes to the language that you want for your ad. Make sure to list this out to help you get started.
3. Media type: You are able to choose a traditional advertisement and all of its format, or you can go with a video that is going to include a button to start the video on the image.
4. Ad destination: This is going to allow you to add in some kind of link to the advertisement. You can link back to your profile page, or another URL based on your needs. If you are trying to drive traffic to the business website, for example, then you will want to add that

URL in there to get people to click on the ad and hopefully get some revenues in the process.

5. Ad design: Now you need to work on the design when it comes to your ad. You want to create a headline and a description. The headline is going to be limited to just 25 characters and your description is 75 characters. Make both short and sweet to get the point across.

6. Ad variations: One of the neat things that you are able to do with LinkedIn is that you can choose from more than one variation for the ads that you want to make. You can choose to add your profile or an external URL. You can choose where you would like it to be located.

   a. Keep in mind that when you are working on LinkedIn, you are working with push advertising rather than pull. What this means is that the audience you are searching for is not really looking for the product you have. this means that you need to be able to make advertisements that will really stand out to people and catch their attention.

The next thing that you need to focus on here is targeting. You need to tell LinkedIn where you would like them to send the ads. Do you have a specific audience in mind. If you don't know about your audience, then it is time to do some research and figure out which group of people you would like to spend your time sending the ad to.

LinkedIn, like the other social media profiles, will allow you to work with a lot of options when it comes to targeting. You can choose your audience based on their gender, their age, where they work, their interests, their family life, where they live, and more. You can add in any kind of targeting that you would like to the mix to help you reach just the right person that you would like.

Before you send the ad out to the world on this site, make sure that you set up the budget that you would like to work with. You need to make sure that you are telling the site how much you are willing to spend for the campaign. You can choose a daily amount that you are comfortable with, or even a whole campaign amount, and let the site know. Think about how much reach you would like to have, and then figure out the budget that works the best to go with this.

LinkedIn may not be the option that a lot of people will think about when it comes to marketing their business. But there are millions of users on this site, and it is a great place for you to really reach the customers that you need, even before they know that they need your product. Doing a bit of organic work and some paid advertising will ensure that you will be able to reach the customers that you need.

Chapter 9: Applying This to Your Business

Now that we have had some time to look at the different types of social media and how they are going to work together, it is time to learn some of the things that you can do to ensure that you can grow your business with social media. You need to make sure that you are able to really take some of the benefits and neat features that come with social media, and implement it into your business, without changing up the way that you provide quality service and more. Some of the things that you can do to ensure that you are properly applying social media to your business, no matter what kind of business it is, includes

Set your goals for social media

Before you ever go to any of the social media sites that we have talked about above, you need to make sure that you have been able to set up some goals for what you want to get out of them. If you just come into it all without a plan and you only start posting random things at random times, and never communicating with your potential customers when they say something or ask a question, then you are gong to end up alienating others, and wasting your time and money.

Having some clear set goals are going to be the best way that you prepare for working on these social media sites. You will know what to post, when to post, how to interact and meet with your customers, and more. This ensures that all of your advertising on these sites, whether it is organic or paid, is going to be as successful as possible.

Always be consistent

You are not going to get the customers that you want if you are not able to stay consistent on the ways that you post online. Your customers are going to get pretty tired of waiting around for your posts if it has been a couple weeks or longer. And it doesn't work to post a bunch one day, and then not post again until a week later, and then have a few good days, and then go silent. There needs to be some consistency to what you are doing if you want any chance of catching the interest of your customers, and keeping it.

When it comes to the posts that you put up, the message that you are sending out, and how often you are on social media, you need to be consistent the whole time. this is truly one of the number one things that will determine if you are actually successful with social media or not.

Your goal here is to make a plan for this. Think ahead to what you would like to post, and how often you would like to do the posting, and then stick with this. It is ideal if you are able to post a few times a day to keep people interested in you, but you have to depend on your goals and your following. But you are not able to go from a schedule of posting once a month and then posting five times a day and then go back to once a month and then wonder why you don't have a following that is engaged in you.

If it is needed, consider sitting down at the beginning of the week, or maybe for a few weeks in advance, and figure out your posting. There are even tools that you are able to work with in order to do the posts for you. You can then list it all out with the content and the times, and then let the app do the posting for you, ensuring that you stay engaged with your customers, and you don't get off your schedule.

Consider the social media site that you want to use

You may find that one social media site works for one company, but it just isn't working for you. And maybe there are those who seem to be on all of the social media sites at once and can keep up with it all, and the thought seems to make you exhausted. The nice thing about this is that you don't need to follow what has worked for others. You need to find what is going to work the best for your needs.

Experiment a bit here and find out where your audience is, and where you are able to serve them best. Yes, everyone can benefit from bringing their business online and using social media. But that doesn't mean that you need to be everywhere all of the time. In fact, you may find that it is best if you are able to stick with about two or three that seems to work the best for you. This allows you to really concentrate on the information that you are posting, and ensures that you can really pay attention to what you are doing there.

In addition, learn to push on the networks that work the best for you. There are going to be some networks that seem to work the best for you compared to the others. When you find that there is a network that seems to work the best for your business, or for the customer that you have, then it is time to push on that network and try to take advantage of that one as much as possible. Take a look at some of the analytics that are available with it, and then change your marketing campaign to fit with that.

Make sure your content is best for each platform.

If you have more than one social media site that you want to work with, make sure that you are careful with the content that you are working with. Maintaining accounts on all of these is going to take some time, and you do not want to post the exact same images, posts, and more on all of them. You have to put in the work to format some content that is meant specifically for each platform that you are on.

For example, if you are working with Instagram, you are going to focus on the pictures, images, and videos to bring the customers in. LinkedIn is going to do better with some longer posts. Memes and videos are going to be great for Facebook. And when it comes to Twitter, you need to work with snappy and short announcements. All of these posts need to be different, even if you happen to be delivering the same message each time.

Double check that your message and content align

The next thing that we need to focus on is making sure that any and all content that you put on social media are going to align with the message you want to send out, the message that comes with your business. It is fine to share something that you find interesting or fun on occasion. But if you are just posting random things all the time, you may stray from your business message too much, confuse your customers, and defeat what you are trying to do on social media.

When it is time to build up your presence on social media, getting follows and likes is going to be a great thing. However, you have to look past the number of responses that you are able to get with your posts. There is a lot of temptation out there for you to just put up posts that get attention, but if no one is working with it and clicking on it, and if it isn't aligning with the message that you want to get out there, then it really isn't doing its job.

If you struggle with this, then it is time to bring someone in who can work on this with you. See if you are able to find someone who can look over your content and double check that it is lining up the way that you want. If the business is bigger, then there should already be someone there to help you with this. If you are the only person running it, then it is time to find a trusted friend or family member, or someone you hire out, who is able to do this for you.

Sometimes, your important content is not going to be that popular

It is tempting to only post up things that get a lot of popularity, or those things you know your customers are going to love. But then there are times when you will need to go through and make sure that you post information that is important, even though it may not be that popular.

You will find that there will sometimes be content that is automatically not going to get you a lot of shares and likes. These may include things like important blog posts, press features, charity posts, and testimonials. These are still important content pieces that need to show up. Without these, you will find that it is really hard to establish the validity that your business has in the market.

Despite how important they are, they are not going to help you get a lot of popularity points, and they don't get a ton of attention. This doesn't mean that you should give up posting it. Yes, these may not be the most popular posts that you put up, but they are going to be the foundation that you need to get your company growing and off the ground.

Learn how to balance your business and popularity

Your professional social media site is meant to be for your business, to help others find out about it and really help it to grow. This is why you need to post some of those things that are not that popular. However, this doesn't mean that you don't need to work on posts in order to get the attention that you want. It is fine to work a bit on getting some popularity, because this gets you the attention, shares, and more, that you need to grow your base.

Simply put, there is nothing wrong with being popular on your own social media site. This can be confusing, but you do need to make sure that you have a good balance in there between growing your business and really looking professional, and making sure that you are popular. You need to have a little bit of both and mix the more fun side that wants to be popular with the side that is informative and serious and is able to boost how reputable your business is overall.

Don't forget some of the organic work to help you.

While we did spend a lot of time talking about all of the great things that you are able to do when it comes to paid advertising on a wide variety of social media platforms, it is also important to work on your organic reach as well. While the organic reach doesn't seem to be as efficient as the paid advertising, you need to spend some time on it. This looks more natural to your customers, and it is going to really make the paid advertising more effective.

There are a lot of different things that you are able to do in order to help you get the organic reach that you are looking for. You can post on a consistent basis, you can make sure that the posts that you are using need to provide a lot of value to your customers, you need to use high quality pictures with your posts (no matter which social media site you are on), and you need to make sure to interact and communicate with your followers. This means that if you have a follower who is commenting on your posts or someone who messages you, you need to make sure to respond back to them in a timely manner.

When you spend this time working on building a relationship with your customers, it is so much easier for you to work with the paid advertising that you want. You will already have a nice relationship with your customers, and that will ensure that your paid advertising budget goes so much further overall.

How your target audience can help you choose the right social media sites

Your target audience is going to be so important with each type of marketing that you do. And it is especially important when you are working on social media. Without this, you are going to waste a lot of time and money trying to figure out which sites to go on, what kind of ads to do, and even how to target the ads that you are using.

Before you even think about joining a social media site, it is a good idea to think through the target audience that you have. hopefully you have been able to do this right from the start, but if not, then it is time to do it now. Think about the perfect customer. If you were able to walk into a large group of people and pick anyone to be your customers, who would that person be. Where would they live, what would they look like, what are some of their interests, their age, their marital life, their education and more.

Figuring out the answers to these questions will ensure that you are able to find the results that you want in the long run. Once you have a good target audience set up, you will be able to go through and pick out the social media site that is going to work the best for you. It also becomes a lot easier to know how to market to them, what kinds of advertisements you need to work with, and more.

Use those analytics

All of the social media sites that are out there are going to offer you some form of analytics. You will have to look at each of them on their own in order to figure things out, but it is still an important thing to spend your time and attention on. This can help you know more about your customers, learn where to find them, and figure out what is working and what isn't with your social media marketing campaign.

You need to check up on these analytics on a regular basis. These are going to show you what works and what doesn't. There are a lot of different options out you can do with each of the social media sites, but not all of them are going to work the best for your needs. Having a good idea of what will work for you, and what doesn't, is exactly what you want to look for when you research your analytics.

In the beginning, you may start out with trying a little bit of everything. This is not a bad thing to do. It allows you to spread out your budget and see what works and what doesn't. If you just put your money towards one thing, and not anything else, and that option doesn't work, then it could be a lot of wasted money along the way. Being able to spread out your budget against a few different options is going to make a big difference.

Once you have a chance to try out a few different options, it is time to check them out. the analytics will allow you to figure out what is working, what may need some adjustments, and what you need to avoid completely because it isn't working for your business or your customers. You need to make sure to do this with each social media site. You may find that something works on one of those sites, and it doesn't work on the other. It all depends on the audience that you are reaching in each part. Having this knowledge and putting it to good use for your needs will make your budgeting for marketing a lot easier.

Social media can be beneficial for each business, but there isn't a one size fits all when it comes to this either. Being able to put it all together, and learning what works and doesn't work for you, is going to be the trick that you need to really get the results that you want. Follow the tips above, and learn how to advertise and market in all of the different options that we talked about throughout this guidebook, and you will be able to get the most out of your social media marketing.

Conclusion

Thank for making it through to the end of *Social Media Marketing and Strategic Guide*, let's hope it was informative and able to provide you with all of the tools you need to achieve your goals whatever they may be.

The next step is to decide where you would like to work on social media. Trying to hit all of the platforms that we talked about above is going to seem overwhelming, and for the most part, it is not necessary. There is usually just a few of those platforms that you will be able to reach your customers through, and you will not need to go further than that. By now, you should have a good idea of the two main, maybe three, social media platforms that are the most interesting and helpful to you, and then move on to starting from there.

This guidebook has provided you with the information that you need to get started on social media and seeing the results that you would like. We looked at how to get onto the accounts, how to do some organic reach that won't cost you anything and can be very powerful, even with all of the noise online, if you do them in the proper manner, and even some of the steps to doing paid advertising as well.

Now that you are prepared and understand the importance of social media and the steps that you need to take in order to get started with your own marketing campaign, make sure that you get started with the help of this guidebook today!

Finally, if you found this book useful in any way, a review is always appreciated!